FRIEN

Robert Moffat (1795–1883), a boy from Scotland, was one of the great pioneers of Christian faith in southern Africa. He travelled by wagon across the veld and made friends with warrior chiefs of the Bechuana and the Matabele people. He had some thrilling adventures along the way.

STORIES OF FAITH AND FAME

BISHOP JIM
Joyce Reason — The Story of James Hannington

CONQUEROR OF DARKNESS
Phyllis Garlick — The Story of Helen Keller

CRUSADER FOR CHRIST
Jean Wilson — The Story of Billy Graham

EVER OPEN DOOR
C. Scott — The Story of Dr Barnardo

FRIEND OF THE CHIEFS
Iris Clinton — The Story of Robert Moffat

FROM SLAVE BOY TO BISHOP
John Milsome — The Story of Samuel Adjai Crowther

GOD'S ARCTIC ADVENTURER
Constance Savery — The Story of William Bompas

GOD'S MADCAP
Nancy E. Robbins — The Story of Amy Carmichael

GOLDEN FOOT
J. R. Batten — The Story of Judson of Burma

HORSEMAN OF THE KING
Cyril Davey — The Story of John Wesley

LADY WITH A LAMP
Cyril Davey — The Story of Florence Nightingale

MILLIONAIRE FOR GOD
J. Erskine — The Story of C. T. Studd

NEVER SAY DIE
Cyril Davey — The Story of Gladys Aylward

NIGHT OF THE SNOWS
R. G. Martin — The Story of Wilfred Grenfell

ON THE CLOUDS TO CHINA
Cyril Davey — The Story of Hudson Taylor

PROPHET OF THE PACIFIC
Margaret Kabell — The Story of John G. Paton

QUAKER CAVALIER
Joyce Reason — The Story of William Penn

SAINT IN THE SLUMS
Cyril Davey — The Story of Kagawa of Japan

SEARCHER FOR GOD
Joyce Reason — The Story of Isobel Kuhn

SLAVE SHIP CAPTAIN
Carolyn Scott — The Story of John Newton

SOUTH SEAS SAILOR
Cecil Northcott — The Story of John Williams

STAR OVER GOBI
Cecil Northcott — The Story of Mildred Cable

THE DOCTOR WHO NEVER GAVE UP
C. Scott — The Story of Dr Ida Scudder

THE HEROINE OF NEWGATE
John Milsome — The Story of Elizabeth Fry

THE MAN WHO FREED SLAVES
Elsie M. Johnson — The Story of William Wilberforce

THE MONK WHO SHOOK THE WORLD
Cyril Davey — The Story of Martin Luther

TO BE A PILGRIM
Joyce Reason — The Story of John Bunyan

TRAIL MAKER
R. V. Latham — The Story of David Livingstone

WHITE QUEEN
Donald McFarlan — The Story of Mary Slessor

WIZARD OF THE GREAT LAKE
Donald McFarlan — The Story of Alexander Mackay

YOUNG MAN IN A HURRY
Iris Clinton — The Story of William Carey

FRIEND OF THE CHIEFS

The Story of Robert Moffat

by
IRIS CLINTON

LUTTERWORTH PRESS
CAMBRIDGE

Lutterworth Press
P.O. Box 60
Cambridge CB1 2NT

British Library Cataloguing in Publication Data available

ISBN 0 7188 2242 0

Copyright © 1975 Iris Clinton

First published 1975 by Lutterworth Press
First paperback edition 1975
Reprinted 1988

Cover illustration by Elissa Vial

Printed and bound in Great Britain by
Cox & Wyman Ltd, Reading

CONTENTS

		page
1	No Use for Softies	7
2	The Cape of Storms	15
3	"Voorwaarts!"	21
4	Scouting for the Chief	28
5	The Murderer's Return	35
6	The Rain-maker	44
7	Rescue	54
8	Flies and Ink	60
9	"Bayete! Bayete!"	65
10	The Kraal of the Lion's Paw	74
11	Welcome Home	81
12	Farewell to the Chief	86
13	The Last Trek	92

1

NO USE FOR SOFTIES

"SEWING is girl's work, Mother. I'm a man."
Twelve-year-old Robert Moffat tossed
back his dark hair, as he faced his mother across
the table in their cottage home in Scotland. It was
four o'clock on a winter afternoon, and already
dark.

"Ye'll no' be a man, Robbie, if ye canna look
after yourself. Ye dinna ken, lad, whar your lot
will be cast."

Reluctantly Robert set to work, longing for the
summer days when he could outswim the other
lads in the rough waters of the Firth of Forth, and
go tramping over the heathery moors as soon as
lessons at the village school were done.

But next year Robert's schooldays were over.
He was sent as a prentice boy to a gardener named
Robertson, who thought that the only way to turn
boys into men was to keep them hard at work
twelve hours a day, six days a week.

"Robert! Robert! get up, you lazy loon, it's
four o'clock. You should have got your spade and
been digging by now."

7

Robert pressed his knuckles into his eyes, and tried to shake himself awake. Surely it could not be morning yet. Everywhere was dark. He pulled on his jacket and went to the tin wash-basin to sluice his face. The water in the jug had frozen solid. His hands were sore with chilblains, and he stamped his feet to start the circulation, as he hurried down the stairs and out into the frosty air. He was hungry, but Mr. Robertson believed in boys doing four hours' hard digging before they came in to breakfast. He had no use for "softies"—he wanted his apprentices to develop strong muscles, and bodies that could withstand heat and cold. Then they could go out into the world as men, strong and fit and ready for anything.

Soon Robert's arms were shooting out of his sleeves, and his trousers were inches short. At night he tumbled into bed dead tired. But now that his schooldays were over, he wanted to learn more. He took a tattered Latin grammar to bed with him, and studied it by candlelight as long as he could keep awake. There was still one more thing to do before he blew out the candle.

"Ye must read your Scripture portion every night. Dinna forget, lad," his mother told him when he left home. Robert kept his promise. Then he blew out the candle, pulled the blanket tight round him, and in a second was sound asleep. It seemed to him only a few minutes before he heard again the hated sound—"Four o'clock, Robert, time you were up."

*   *   *

When he was sixteen, Robert got a job in the gardens of the Earl of Moray at Donibristle.

One evening there was a shout down on the shore. "Help! Help! man drowning." Moffat ran full pelt along the beach, tore off his jacket, and plunged in. There was a strong current running, and Moffat had a hard struggle before he brought the terrified young prentice gardener safely to shore.

*   *   *

Two years later, the garden boys on the estate gathered round him to say good-bye, for Robert had got promotion.

"I wonder how you'll like it in England," said one of the boys. "It's an awfu' long journey. My brother went there once, and he was on the sea for twelve days from Greenock to Liverpool."

"Watch out for the Press Gang, Robert," said one of the older men. "You're big and strong—just the sort of lad they'd like in the Navy. They're short of men to fight Napoleon."

The little ship left Greenock in the teeth of a gale. Robert found himself clinging to the ship's rail, cold and soaked to the skin, so sick, that for all he cared the ship could sink with him on it. In a few days the sun shone again, and he began to enjoy his trip.

"What will you do when you leave the ship, Moffat?" asked the Captain as they neared Liverpool.

"Find my way to High Legh, near Knutsford, sir. I've got a post there as gardener."

"That's twenty-six miles away," said the Captain. "I'll book a seat on the coach for you, lad. It'll cost you six shillings."

Robert counted his money and shook his head. "Thank you, sir," he said. "But six shillings is half a week's pay. I can easily walk it."

*　　　*　　　*

"This is real comfort," said Robert, as he looked round his gardener's room on the High Legh estate. It was only one room, in between the potting shed and the tool house, but it had a table, a bench, a paraffin lamp, and a bed with a lumpy mattress and two blankets. He put his Bible and Latin grammar and arithmetic book on the table, his violin case away under the bed, and his Sunday coat, clean shirt and socks in the kit-box which had come down by coach, and his unpacking was complete.

Six thousand miles away, another man was unpacking his belongings in a new hut. His possessions were a skin rug, some beads and a pocket knife. Robert Moffat, the Scots gardener, and Afrikaner, the Hottentot chieftain, did not know that one day their paths would meet. It was in Liverpool that the trail which was to lead them to each other began.

One day a friend came to admire Robert's daffodils. "They're the finest blooms I've ever seen in these parts, Mr. Moffat," he exclaimed. Before he left, he said, "We're having a grand service in our church on Sunday. Will you come with me?"

That service was Robert's first step along the trail. He had learnt his Shorter Catechism at school in Scotland, when the teacher beat him with a strap if he got his answers wrong. But that night he found that Jesus had something to say directly to him, Robert Moffat, and he promised that, with God's help, he would love and serve and follow Him from that day on.

"All men are God's children, Robert," his new friend reminded him. "But there are thousands who have never heard about Him." Robert thought about them sometimes as he trimmed his hedges and pruned his roses. He wondered how they spoke and what they looked like.

At that moment, unknown to Robert, Chief Afrikaner was on the war-path, shooting men who opposed him, burning down African villages, and dragging men, women and children along to the white slave-trader.

*　　*　　*

One day Robert passed a battered poster pasted on a wall. It advertised a missionary meeting, but it was already out of date. "I wish I'd known about it in time," thought Robert. "I'd like to have gone."

Then another thought came to him. "I'll go and see the chairman," he decided. "His name's on the poster, Rev. W. Roby. I'll tell him I'm interested, and ask him what happened."

Robert came out from the chairman's study determined to be a missionary. "You'll have to study and pass your examination first," Mr. Roby had said. Robert was ready. He gave up his head-gardener's job, where he was now earning fifteen shillings a week, and found a post in Manchester. He got less money, but Mr. Smith, his employer, let him have Saturdays free, so that he could go to lectures and qualify himself for the examination.

Mr. Smith's daughter, Mary, was interested in his plans. "I wish you could come with me, Mary," he said.

"I wish I could, Robert. But Father says we shall never see you again once you go to Africa. If you escape the savages, you'll be eaten by the lions or die of thirst in the desert, and he forbids me to go. It's bad enough to lose you, he says, and he is not going to lose me too. I'm his only daughter."

"I know, Mary," said Robert. "Perhaps if I can make a home for you when I get there, your father will let you come."

"I hope so," said Mary. "Anyhow I am coming to London to see you farewelled."

There had been a farewell service in Manchester for the new missionaries of the London Missionary Society, but the service in London was more impressive still. Robert Moffat, a tall young man of twenty, stood with four other young men going to Africa, and four who were going to the South Seas. One of these was John Williams, who was clubbed to death by savages on the island of Erromanga.

The presiding minister handed to each of them a Bible, saying:

"Go, our beloved brethren, and live agreeably to this word, and publish the Gospel of our Lord

Jesus Christ to the heathen, according to your calling, gifts and abilities, in the name of the Father and of the Son and of the Holy Ghost." Robert joined solemnly in the reply, "I will, God being my helper."

A few days later, on October 20, 1816, the *Alacrity* moved out with the tide, and hoisted sail. On board was Robert Moffat, bound for new trails in Africa.

2

THE CAPE OF STORMS

"PHEW," said Robert Moffat, wiping his face with a large handkerchief, "it's hot." The sailing ship *Alacrity* had taken eighty-six days to do the voyage from England to South Africa, and Moffat landed in January, which was midsummer in Cape Town.

He looked around him. There was the fort, built by the East India Company in the shape of their crest, a five-pointed star. Towering above him was Table Mountain with its queer flat top. "Look," said the friend who had come to meet the new missionary, "the old grey mountain has got his table-cloth on in your honour," and Moffat watched the thick cloud that hung down over the top like a white cloth.

As they walked up the street, Moffat looked at the cool white single-storey houses, roofed with slate or thatch, their gardens a blaze of brightly coloured flowers. He saw brown-skinned men working in the gardens, and a big native woman

15

with a bright coloured turban guiding a small white toddler up the path.

"Are they slaves?" asked Moffat.

"Yes. We all have native servants here, and most of them are slaves."

Robert was glad when they turned in through a garden gate, and sat down on a cool stone seat on the shady stoep with the green leaves of a grape vine above them. A servant brought out a dish of early grapes. "Try these, Mr. Moffat," said his host. "They were picked a few minutes ago. You'll find them refreshing."

Robert had been so long at sea that the ground still seemed to be rocking under his feet, but he did not want to sit still for long—there was too much to see.

"Voorwaarts! voorwaarts!"—he heard the words, and the crack of a whip which accompanied them. There was a creaking, lumbering sound, and a long span of sixteen large red oxen passed down the road. Their curving horns and humped backs gave them a proud look. They plodded along at walking pace, pulling a large covered wagon.

Robert wrote home to Mary to tell her his experiences. "There are many natives here in Cape Town," he told her. "But I am appointed to carry the Gospel to the kraal of a Hottentot chief named Afrikaner, who lives beyond the bounds of the Colony. They say here that he is a murderer, and the Governor has put a price on his head. Pray for me, Mary, that I may win the heart of this savage."

*   *   *

Moffat had to spend eight months in the Cape, before the Governor would allow him to go beyond the bounds of the Colony to Afrikaner. He set to work to learn Dutch, and found that his Scots tongue helped him to pronounce the words. Then he learnt to ride, and set out to visit the lonely frontier farms. He carried a water-bottle and food for the journey—a blanket and his Bible in the saddle-bags.

Grasses, which reached up to the saddle, swished and parted as the horse pushed its way through. Light-footed springbok leapt into the air with fright, and cleared ant-heaps and boulders as they sprang into safety. Once he heard the low roar of a lion. He rode through fields of mealies and pumpkins, and orchards of peach and apricot, to a farmhouse. Long before he reached the house, the farmer and his family came out to meet him. It was three months since they had seen another white man, and soon Moffat was sitting down to a meal of mutton roasted in the pot, with home-grown pumpkin, potatoes and mealies, melk tart made of milk and eggs from the farm, and flour ground by the farmer. "We grow and make all we need," said the farmer's wife.

One of the farmer's sons offered Moffat a strip of something dark that looked like twisted rope. "No, thank you," said Moffat. "I do not chew tobacco."

Piet laughed. "Mynheer Moffat thinks biltong is tobacco," he said.

"You will need to make biltong if you travel in this country, Mynheer," said the farmer. "When you kill an animal, you must hang up strips of the meat to dry hard in the sun. Then you can chew it when you are on trek, and it will keep away hunger for a long time, and give you strength."

The big Dutch Bible stood by itself on a table with a neat white cloth. When darkness fell, the farmer placed the Book reverently before Moffat. His sons and daughters gathered round. "We will have a proper service tonight," he said. "Mynheer will read and speak to us."

Moffat looked at the expectant white faces in front of him. He remembered the men and women he had seen in the fields, in the kitchen, and about the house.

"Where are the servants?" he asked.

The farmer stared at Moffat in amazement. Ah

well, he was a young man, only a few years older than Piet, his youngest son. He was a stranger too, and new to the ways of the country.

"You mean the Hottentots?" asked the farmer. "Why, man, you might as well call in the dogs or the baboons as call in the Hottentots. They are like the dogs—they would not understand."

Moffat went quietly on with the service. He opened the big family Bible at the fifteenth chapter of Matthew, and read the conversation between Jesus and the Syro-Phoenician woman. "Yet the dogs eat of the crumbs which fall from their masters' table," said the woman to Jesus.

"Stop! Stop!" said the old farmer. "Piet, go out to the fields and fetch in the Hottentots. You have taken a hard stone, young man," he said to Moffat, "to break a hard head."

*　　*　　*

It was an exciting day for Moffat when he climbed into his wagon and started his trek to the murderer's kraal. He knew now how to repair a wagon-wheel, how to yoke and unyoke the ox-team, how to shoot and cook for the pot, and how to make himself understood in the Dutch language.

As they out-spanned the first night and Moffat drank a mug of coffee boiled on the camp fire, under the velvety, star-lit African sky, he was glad to be on his way at last. The natives were just dropping off to sleep by the fire when they heard a strange sound. They sat up to listen. From inside the wagon came the booming of a strong bass voice.

> "Awake my soul in joyful lays
> To sing my great Redeemer's praise,"

sang Moffat. It was a favourite hymn of his mother's. He thought how his mother, and Mary Smith, would be praying for him on his great adventure. "O God, help me to be faithful," he prayed.

3

"VOORWAARTS!"

"HE'LL skin you alive, and make your skin into a drum." The missionary wagon had halted outside a farmhouse to fill up the water containers. "Where are you making for?" the farmer had asked.

"Afrikaner's kraal," answered Moffat.

"Man," said the farmer, "you don't know what you're doing. He shot my brother dead."

"He killed my two sons," added another. "Turn back while you can, Mynheer. You are too young to die."

"It is the path to which God has called me," said Moffat simply.

The oxen were watered, the jars filled, Moffat had drunk coffee with his hosts.

"Voorwaarts!" he cried, and the wagon rolled away in a cloud of desert dust.

*   *   *

"If only I could see just one blade of grass," said Moffat. Everywhere was sand—even the thorn bushes were grey with it. The river beds were dry and stony—there was no drop of water anywhere.

As the wagon crept slowly over three hundred miles of desert, Moffat thought of what an older missionary had told him about Afrikaner—how he had been cheated and betrayed by a Dutch farmer, and had turned bandit. He pegged his victims to the ground and left them for the ants to eat. He had burnt and destroyed the mission station at Warm Bath. How would he treat this new missionary?

They travelled by night to avoid the fierce heat of the sun. The team of sixteen oxen strained and pulled the wagon through the deep sand. At last the big iron-bound wooden wheels sank deep into a drift and stuck. The oxen heaved, the Hottentot driver cracked his whip across their flanks, Moffat put his shoulder to the wheel and strained till he felt his muscles would burst. Still the wagon stood fast.

The oxen lay down in their traces, panting with heat and thirst.

They let the animals free. Soon the sand was beginning to burn even their tough hides. They crowded against one another, to try and take shelter in the shade of each other's bodies. They bellowed with pain as they put their hooves down in the burning sand.

Moffat was so exhausted that he wanted to lie down like the oxen. But he dared not risk the animals dying from thirst. They *must* have water. He took a spade and walked forward into the desert.

"I'll dig for water," he said. Sweat ran from him as he dug in the loose sand. Three feet, four feet, he went down. "Look out!" He heard the warning shout just in time to leap aside as an ox, maddened by thirst, rushed towards the hole. He had smelt water. He had one lick of slimy green water before the sides of the hole caved in. The rest of the oxen stampeded towards it. Once again Moffat had to dig.

*　　*　　*

Some weeks later brown-skinned men, with waistbelts of leopard-skin fringed with long monkey-tails, came leaping and prancing towards the wagon. They yelled and shrieked as they sprang high into the air, their tails flying out behind them. "They are trying to frighten me," thought Moffat. "I must be near the Chief's kraal."

The driver was afraid, but Moffat urged him on with a cheery "Voorwaarts!"

Soon he saw ahead of him a little cluster of bee-hive-shaped huts. The monkey-tailed warriors were still prancing ahead, as the wagon came to a

23

halt. The Chief's brother, Titus the straight-shooter, led the wagon some distance away. "The Chief will see you later," he said.

Moffat stood his ground. An hour later Afrikaner came out of his hut. He looked the new missionary up and down. "You are young," he said. "That is good. You will be able to stay a long time with my people."

Then he shouted an order, and immediately women of the tribe ran forward. They were naked except for skirts made of skins, sewn together with animal sinews. The women had never seen soap, and the skirts had never been washed. Moffat turned his head away to avoid the smell. Then he pulled himself together. "I am here to tell them of God's love," he thought. "I must not let a smell prevent me."

Each woman carried a grass mat and a long, pointed stick. They stuck the sticks in the ground in a circle, bent them towards each other, tied them together at the top, fastened the mats on to them, and in half an hour the missionary's home was complete.

Afrikaner took time to sum up the new missionary. He watched him when a pair of angry bulls, fighting in the night, smashed in his hut. Moffat did not shout or swear, but quietly set to work to mend the gash. Meat was scarce and no

one knew how to grow corn or vegetables.
Afrikaner noticed how this dark-haired, black-
bearded young man grew thin as he kept going on
a drink of milk three times a day. He saw him pull
his belt a little tighter each day to stop the hungry
feeling just as Afrikaner's own people did. Still he
did not complain. At night Moffat took his
precious violin and sat on a flat rock near his hut
and played the old psalm tunes to himself, and
sang an evening hymn.

Little by little Afrikaner came to trust him.
Moffat collected the children round him, and began to teach them. "They would learn better if
they were clean, Chief," said Moffat. "They are
always scratching, and their arms and legs are full
of sores."

"Then you and I will wash them," said Afrikaner. He and Moffat took a hundred small children down to the spring, and gave them their first
scrub. Then back went the dirty animal skins on
to their clean bodies.

"We must wash the karosses too," said Moffat.
They began all over again, making the children
wash the filthy skin skirts and blankets.

"I wish Mary was here," thought Moffat.
"She would make cotton frocks and shirts for
them, and they would be easy to wash, not like
these greasy, dirty skins."

"You must teach me too, Mynheer," said Afrikaner one night. Afrikaner had learnt to speak Dutch. Now Moffat taught him to read his Dutch Bible. "This is good teaching, Mynheer," he said, as bit by bit he thumbed his way through a Gospel. "My head is so small and these things are so big. I have heard the Lord say, 'This is my way. Walk ye in it.' Pray for me, Mynheer, that I may learn and follow the way."

*　　　*　　　*

Afrikaner and his people were often hungry. Nothing but thorn bushes grew in the rocky, sandy soil. The few sheep were lean and scraggy, and the under-nourished cattle yielded little milk.

"Why don't you find a new place to live, Afrikaner?" Moffat asked him. "Somewhere where you could grow crops, and where you would have water?"

"I have so many enemies, my father," said the Chief. "I cannot go far. Will Mynheer take his wagon and come with me?"

"I am no blacksmith," said Moffat. "The wagon needs a new iron rim for the wheel. But if you will kill two goats and keep the skins whole and make them soft, in the way of your people, then I will see if I can make a pair of bellows and heat the iron for welding."

"Oow!" shouted the natives with delight, watching the iron grow white-hot in the flame as Moffat worked away at his home-made bellows, the sweat streaming down his face and hissing in the fire.

When the wagon was ready, it did not take Moffat long to make his own preparations.

His legs stuck out of his trousers, and his arms out of his jacket sleeves, because he was still growing.

"You were right, Mother," he said to himself as he sat on a rock outside his hut, mending the shirt which he had torn into holes on a thorn bush.

That journey was unsuccessful, and so were the following ones. And then came a journey that Moffat never forgot.

4

SCOUTING FOR THE CHIEF

MOFFAT and Afrikaner found no good land for the tribe to the north of Vredeberg, the Chief's kraal. Moffat decided to see what lay to the east.

"Perhaps somewhere between here and Griqua-town there may be good land where you could settle and live at peace," he said to Afrikaner.

With Moffat went Jantje Vanderbyl, a guide who was used to the desert, two of the Chief's brothers, and his son Jonker. They took eight horses with them. Each man had a sheepskin blanket called a kaross. They took no food. They would shoot that on the way, or get it from natives on the road.

Their course ran beside the Orange River, which wound like a serpent through a desert of thorn and mimosa bush. They rode as much as possible by night, making their way through pathless scrub and thorn bushes which tore pieces out of their clothes and skins.

One night they camped above a river-bank.

They dared not light a fire in case Bushmen with their poisoned arrows and blow-pipes might be hiding in the bush. The night wind blew cold, and they had left their karosses with the horses.

Moffat began to dig in the sand. He wriggled down the hole, leaving only his head sticking out. "This is good," he said, "I'm warm and comfortable." "What if the lions come?" asked one of the others. "Lions won't worry about heads if they can get whole bodies," laughed Moffat, and settled down to a good night's sleep.

*   *   *

Although there was water in the river-bed, the country on each side was scorched brown by the sun, and as hot as an oven. They had ridden all morning across the burning plain. In the early afternoon Moffat saw a small pool of water near the main stream and lay down to drink. Immediately he felt a strange taste in his mouth. Then to his horror he noticed a rough fence round the pool, and realized it was a Bushman game trap. The tiny Bushmen who lived in the desert had poisoned the water with bulbs and roots to trap any animal who went to drink. At that moment a little Bushman ran up to him. Terrified, he seized Moffat by the hand to lead him away from the water. Moffat felt as if his whole body was swelling up within him—his pulses raced—he was too giddy to stand. Other Bushmen gathered round, and made strange clicks and grunts to express their sorrow. Moffat managed to summon up a smile in reply. When they saw him smile, they capered with joy, and clicked more loudly than ever.

By next day the effect of the poison had worn off. As they left, Moffat gave the Bushmen some tobacco, which set them dancing for joy.

"I wish I could speak to them about Him who came to redeem the poor and needy," said Moffat. "But I know no word of their language, nor they of mine."

Some days later, they began to trek away from the bed of the Orange River towards the mission station at Griquatown. It was unknown country. They had enough meat left to give them a few mouthfuls each and they decided to save this till the next day. They had nothing in which to carry water on horseback. Moffat copied the natives, and filled himself up with water before mounting his horse in the morning. That gave him a comfortably full feeling all day, and prevented him from realizing how hungry he was.

At night they came to an abandoned hut. There were jackal and hyena tracks going in and out, and from the distant river the hippopotami kept up a blowing and snorting chorus. But the party were too tired to care.

"Before we sleep, brothers, let us sing our evening hymn," said Moffat, and they sang together:

> "Come, Thou fount of every blessing,
> Tune my heart to sing Thy grace:
> Streams of mercy never ceasing
> Call for songs of loudest praise."

*　　　*　　　*

By next evening, weak with hunger and thirst, they found the going hard. Vanderbyl and Moffat were on ahead. They glanced back, and saw the other three men staying behind.

"They're lighting their pipes. They'll soon catch us up," said Vanderbyl, and he and Moffat rode on. After a little while they halted and hallooed. All was silent. They fired shots into the air. The last one was answered by a lion close at hand.

They ran to their horses and re-mounted, urging them up the steep hill side to a place where they could pelt the lion with stones. But the rock ledge proved too narrow for them to stand on, and there were no loose stones. The terrified horses stumbled back down the path with the lion on their tracks. The towering cliffs, and the grunt of an old baboon, added to the eeriness of the scene.

Hour after hour they rode—till they reached a small hill and could go no further. They knelt and thanked God for their safety, pillowed their heads on their saddles, and slept, in spite of the distant roar of the lion.

Next morning Moffat climbed the hill to look for water, but he could see nothing but earth scorched dry by the sun. As he scrambled down, he coughed. Instantly a horde of gigantic baboons surrounded him. They grunted, grinned, and sprang from stone to stone, sticking out their ugly mouths and drawing back the skin of their foreheads, threatening attack. Moffat tried to keep them off with his loaded gun. He dared not fire, for he knew that, if he wounded one of them, the rest would skin him alive in five minutes. They followed him all the way down—one big one putting out his hand to touch Moffat's hat.

Vanderbyl stood waiting at the foot of the hill with the horses. Moffat could not speak, his throat and lips were too dry, but he signed to the guide that he had not found water.

Slowly they made their way on. Suddenly

before their eyes danced the blue waters of a lovely lake. Trees were reflected in its clear depths. Little bays and islands appeared—Moffat could see a small boat moving on the waves. They urged on the horses. Water! Water! After another hour's riding, the horrid truth dawned on them. It was a mirage, caused by the sun's rays on the burning sand.

*　　　*　　　*

Two days later, speechless and haggard, they arrived at the house of Mr. Anderson, the missionary at Griquatown. He stared at them in amazement as they stood at the door, covered with dust and sweat. They made themselves understood by signs. Mrs. Anderson quickly prepared coffee and a little food. It was three days since they had eaten.

The travellers stayed for some days at the mission house, and the three missing members of the party followed them there.

Moffat enjoyed being able to speak freely in his own language once more. He rejoiced too in seeing the attentive congregation listening to the missionaries.

"I bring you greetings from your Christian brothers at Afrikaner's kraal," said Moffat. "The Griquas too are learning to love their Lord."

Mr. Anderson took Moffat on a visit to an outpost on the Kuruman River. "There is a spring of water near here that never runs dry," he said. "The people call it 'The Eye of Kuruman.' "

"That would be a good place for a mission station," Moffat remarked.

"It has refreshed our souls and bodies to stay here with you," he said to the Andersons when they were ready to leave.

"God go with you all," said the missionaries, waving good-bye.

5

THE MURDERER'S RETURN

"I WANT you to come to Cape Town with me, Afrikaner," said Moffat suddenly one day. He had been back for some weeks from his scouting trip. Afrikaner was not prepared to move his tribe to the spring at Kuruman, and Moffat could report on no other suitable site. "You and your tribe will starve if you cannot get supplies from the Colony. As long as you are an outlaw, there is no chance of contact with the Cape. Besides, there is another reason, Chief."

Afrikaner was speechless with amazement. His eyes rolled in his head.

At last he gasped out: "Mynheer, I thought you were my friend. Do you want to see me hung up on a gibbet at Cape Town? There is a reward of a thousand dollars on my head."

"You have not heard the other reason, Chief," said Moffat quietly. "I have told them in the Cape that Chief Afrikaner is now a Christian: he does not plunder or murder any more—but they will not believe it. Come with me, Afrikaner, to prove

35

to them that they are wrong. They will not believe unless they see you."

Afrikaner sat in thought. Then he said, "I will go away and consider, Mynheer, and ask God to guide me."

*　　*　　*

For three days tongues buzzed in the kraal. Some of the old men were angry. "You cannot do this to our Chief," they said. "You teach him the Christian way, and then you take him down to Cape Town to be hung. That is not right."

Then Afrikaner himself sought out Moffat in his hut. "I will come with you, Mynheer," he said. "It is the way of God."

Moffat put his hand on the Chief's shoulder. "That is the bravest thing you have ever done, Chief," he said. "Now let us make our plans."

Moffat was sure that once he had got Afrikaner safely to Cape Town the Governor would cancel the price on the outlaw's head, and receive him into favour. But there were the dangers of the journey to be overcome. Many of the farmers knew Afrikaner, and would shoot him at sight.

"You will need a disguise," said the missionary. "The safest way will be for you to go as my servant. I will lend you clothes. The farmers won't take any notice of a servant."

The Chief agreed. He put on an old pair of leather trousers, and Moffat gave him a shirt. He wore an old battered hat, and a ragged duffel jacket. Moffat's dress was not much better, and his skin was tanned brown in the sun, but his features and his speech marked him as a European.

There were anxious faces in Vredeberg as Moffat and the Chief set out in the wagon.

"Do not fear," said Moffat. "Your Chief will come back to you alive and no longer an outlaw. God be with you all."

On the way they passed a bare patch of ground, where there were still traces of charred wood, and rocks scarred by fire. Afrikaner's face grew sad.

"That was the mission station of Warm Bath, Mynheer. In the old days I burnt it to the ground. Many lost their lives that day. I pursued the fugitives, and fought with them."

Presently they came to a neat and tidy village, and heard the sound of a hymn coming from a tiny school-house. An elderly African came out to greet them. He took one look at Moffat's servant and stretched out his hand. "Afrikaner—greetings, brother. You and I have changed since last we met."

Afrikaner's voice shook. "Mynheer," he said to Moffat, "this man fled from Warm Bath when I burnt it. I pursued him and we fought. I had a gun and he had a spear. I thought I had shot him dead."

"I thought I had mortally wounded you," replied the man. "Come, Afrikaner, I have heard that you now follow the Christian God, and so do I. We built this place after you destroyed Warm Bath. Come and meet your old enemies, and let us talk and eat together, and give thanks to God who has saved us all."

*   *   *

As they journeyed on, they had to stop at lonely farmhouses for water, for there were no water-holes along the desert path. "We will go to that farm on the hill," said Moffat. "I know the farmer there. He and his wife were kind to me on my journey up." They out-spanned the wagon. "Jump down, boy," said Moffat to Afrikaner, with a twinkle in his eye. Afrikaner enjoyed the joke. "Ja, Mynheer," he smiled.

Leaving the wagon in charge of the Hottentot servants, Moffat walked up to the farmhouse to ask for water for men and cattle. The farmer came down the hill to meet the visitor. "Môre,

Mynheer!" called out Moffat, holding out his hand in greeting.

"Moffat!" cried the farmer. "Don't come near me. You are a ghost. I know it. You were murdered long ago by Afrikaner. Everybody says you were murdered. I met a man who saw your bones."

Moffat showed the farmer his strong right hand. "This doesn't belong to a ghost," he said.

"Quick!" said the farmer, "my wife's coming. She's afraid of spooks. Let us move over to the wagon out of her sight."

At the wagon, the farmer stretched out a trembling hand. "When did you rise from the dead, Mynheer?" he asked.

"I'm no ghost, man," said Moffat. "Afrikaner is a good man now."

The farmer pointed to his forehead. "Mynheer has had a touch of the sun, perhaps," he said sympathetically. "He does not know what he is saying. Why, if it was really true, I would go any distance with you to see him, even though he killed my uncle."

Afrikaner was standing respectfully behind Moffat, like a servant.

"Do you really wish to see the Chief?" asked Moffat.

"If he is now as you say," replied the farmer.

Moffat stepped aside, so that Afrikaner was in full view.

"Here then," he said, "is Afrikaner."

Afrikaner took off his old felt hat, and bowed low. The farmer was thunderstruck. Then he called his wife and family. "See a miracle," he said to them. "O God, what cannot Thy grace accomplish?"

"Do not spread the news that Afrikaner is with me," said Moffat as they left. "I do not want his enemies to track him down before we reach Cape Town."

*　　*　　*

Afrikaner was saddened as he heard at farm after farm how men had lived in terror of him. The farmers spoke freely to Moffat about him, little knowing that it was the Chief himself who was standing silent behind the missionary. Even the Governor at Cape Town, Lord Charles Somerset, doubted Moffat's story, but promised that he would receive the Chief.

Not till Afrikaner stood before him in person and spoke of his new way of life did the Governor believe. He looked with interest at the Chief's well-worn Bible.

"I kept you here for eight months when first

you landed, Mr. Moffat," said the Governor. "I did not want missionaries to go beyond the Colony, for I was afraid that this man and his followers would kill them. I did not believe that missionaries could change the hearts of savages. Now I have seen it for myself. Afrikaner, you are an outlaw no longer."

"And the price on my head, Excellency?" asked the Chief.

"We will find a better use for that," he said. "You need goods for your people. I will give you a strong wagon and a team of oxen worth that same sum, to take you and your goods safely back to your people."

Moffat looked forward to the journey back to Vredeberg with Afrikaner. There was no need now for the Chief to travel in disguise. He carried the Governor's pardon, and news of that would spread along the frontier farms ahead of them.

But Moffat found other plans awaiting him. "We want you now to carry the Gospel to the Bechuanas, Mr. Moffat," said the Directors of the Mission in Cape Town.

"My work lies with Chief Afrikaner," said Moffat.

"My heart is heavy, Mynheer," said the Chief. "My people will be full of sorrow if I return without you. But if the Bechuana need you, you must go to them, and teach them too the right way. Do not worry about your goods, Mynheer. I myself will move your wooden chest with the brass locks and your name on the lid, and will take it to Lattakoo for you. Nothing of yours will be lost."

Moffat watched Afrikaner and his men go off without him in the wagon which the Governor had given them, while he remained in Cape Town for the final preparations to be made for the mission in Lattakoo. It was a sad and lonely time for Moffat, till one day a messenger brought him a letter.

He had seen a ship put into Table Bay, and wondered whether there would be any letters for him on board. He broke the seal quickly—it was from Mary Smith.

"My parents have given their consent at last for me to come to Africa," she wrote. "I shall travel on the next ship, and we can be married in Cape Town."

Respectable people stared with amazement as they saw a tall young man with a black beard tearing along the pavement to a minister's house.

"Whatever's the matter with him? Is he mad or is someone ill and he's fetching the doctor?"

"No," laughed a neighbour. "That's young Mr. Moffat the missionary. He's just heard that his bride is coming from England and he's running to the minister to make arrangements for the wedding. He likes to do things thoroughly, and in good time."

6

THE RAIN-MAKER

"HERE is our new home, Mary," said Moffat. Her first home had been the wagon in which they had travelled for three months since their wedding in Cape Town. She had grown quite fond of the lumbering old wagon. She took one last look round—there in one corner was the bed made of latticed thongs, with a box underneath for their spare clothing; Robert's shirts and her dresses. A shelf ran along one side, with a raised edge to it, so that things would not fall off it as the wagon lurched and bumped along through the bush. A brass-bound water barrel stood in one corner, and the barrel which held the supply of powder for the guns in another. There was a leopard-skin rug on the floor, and a vase made from an animal's horn on the wall. Mary had picked yellow mimosa from a bush and put it in the vase.

She could have enjoyed the wagon journey if it had not been for the terrible heat, the dust and the flies. But now the journey was over—they had arrived at Lattakoo, their new home.

Scattered among the dusty thorn bushes were hundreds of squat little beehive huts where the Bechuana people lived. The huts were blackened, and the people had sore eyes, from the smoke of the cooking fires. The men wore filthy sheep-skins, and the women smeared their bodies with red ochre, so that if one of them brushed against Mary a red smear appeared on her dress.

"There is much work to do for the Lord here, Mary," said Robert. Mary agreed. She was just as keen to begin work as Robert was.

*   *   *

Soon the native drums began to roll. "That's for us, Mary," said Moffat. "That is a summons from King Mothibi. We have got to go and pay him our respects."

They walked across to the Chief's kraal. There, on a stool in front of his royal hut, sat King Mothibi. He wore a leopard-skin over his shoulders, a girdle of ostrich feathers round his waist, and a leopard's tail hanging from his belt behind. His face and body were painted with red ochre. On one side of him stood a big fat native woman, the Queen, Mahuto, and with her an erect young native boy, the Chief's eldest son, Peclo.

Sweat ran down the Chief's face as he wore all

his finery in the heat of the mid-day sun. Moffat's
thermometer had shown a shade temperature of
120° at noon.

A servant bowed before the Chief, and offered
him a basket of dried cow dung. Mothibi took
some, and wiped his hands on it. Then the basket
was passed round, and Queen Mahuto, Robert
and Mary took from it, and wiped their hands.

Then the Chief poured thick sour milk out of
a goat-skin bag into a reed bowl. He drank
noisily, then passed the bowl to his guests. Moffat
was proud of the brave face Mary put on it when
it was her turn to drink, but he took it from her as
soon as he could, and drank noisily himself to
show respect to the king.

Mahuto put her face close to Mary and began
to talk very quickly. "What is she saying?"
Robert asked the interpreter. "She wants a
present," he answered. Moffat sent for a package
from the wagon. He opened it, and took out three
yards of bright red cloth for Mahuto. She swung
her hips and smiled from ear to ear with pride
and pleasure as she draped it round her shoulders.

"We have had our official welcome, Mary,"
said Robert. "Now we must get to work."

"Do you think Afrikaner will bring those goods
which you left with him?" Mary asked him. "You
are needing the books and tools. Several people in

Cape Town told me you were foolish to trust him. They said you would never see your tools again."

"Afrikaner knows that Christians keep their promises," said Moffat. "He will bring them."

Mary went back into the mission house, which had a living room and a bedroom, and a hut for a kitchen in the yard behind. A crowd of native men and women followed her in, laughing and chattering. One woman seized her arm and rolled up her sleeve, to see if she was really white all over. Some sat on her chairs, and some lolled against the white-washed walls, leaving them streaked with red. When they grew tired they trooped off, carrying some of Mary's spoons and ornaments away with them. When they had gone Mary saw with horror bugs climbing up her walls, and fleas hopping over the floor.

She stepped outside for a breath of air. In the distance she noticed a cloud of dust. "Robert!" she called. "Someone is coming." Robert was busy digging—he knew that he and Mary would starve unless he could raise some crops.

Together they watched, as the cloud came nearer. Then Moffat gave a shout of delight. "It's Afrikaner, Mary," he said. "I knew he would not fail us."

The Chief's wagon rolled up to the missionary's hut, and Moffat and Afrikaner grasped each other by the hand. "I have brought your goods," said the Chief. "Will Mynheer check them and see that nothing is missing?"

"Nothing is missing, Chief. They are all here."

Afrikaner was overjoyed to see Moffat again. "I will bring my people to. live here too," he said. "Then Mynheer can teach us all."

Afrikaner knelt once more in prayer, and he and Moffat and Mary took communion together.

"God be with you, brother," said Moffat as the Chief rode away again. "I shall come back, if He wills," said Afrikaner. It was with a sad heart that Moffat heard many months later that Afrikaner had been taken ill soon after he reached home, and had died, so that Moffat would not see him again at Lattakoo.

*   *   *

One evening Moffat came home tired and disappointed. With him was Robert Hamilton, his fellow missionary, a builder and handy-man.

Mary brought in the candles which she herself had made by dipping a reed in fat melted down from a sheep's tail. Moffat had killed the sheep, and she had cut it up into joints. She had cut strips from it and hung them in the sun to dry for biltong. She had salted down other parts to preserve them, and tried to find a place to store them that would be safe from ants and wild animals. That one sheep would have to last them a long time.

As they sat down to eat their mutton chops, cooked over a wood fire, Mary could see that Robert was worried.

"We're not making any headway," he said at last. "Lying and thieving is going on all round us."

"If only I could talk to them in their own language!" said Moffat. "I am sure the interpreter makes mistakes. Yesterday I said 'The salvation of the soul is a very important matter.' He interpreted it into Sechuana and the people just rocked with laughter. I think he got the word wrong. 'Zaak' means matter. I believe he thought I said 'zak'."

"But that means 'bag', doesn't it?" said Mary.

"Yes," said Robert. "No wonder they laughed if he translated it 'The salvation of the soul is a great big bag.' I must learn the language, but there is so much to do."

"No one can live here much longer unless the rain comes," said Hamilton. "There has been no rain for five years now."

"Chief Mothibi told me he has sent for one of the best rain-makers. He expects him here tomorrow."

*　　　*　　　*

49

Shouting and laughter and the sound of hurrying feet came from all directions. Moffat called to one of the men running by.

"We are going down to the spring, Mynheer. The rain-maker is on his way, and he has sent a messenger to say we must all wash our feet, else he cannot make rain."

He was an impressive figure when he arrived next day, with his ostrich feather headdress and his cloak of leopard-skin and monkey-tails. He ordered the people to give him sheep and goats. A few drops of rain fell and were gone again. "You only give me sheep and goats to kill, so I can only make goat-rain; give me fat, slaughter oxen, and I will let you see ox-rain."

Still no rain fell.

The rain-maker kept playing for time.

"You must bring me a lion's heart," he said. The men trooped to the forest and hunted down a lion and brought him the heart. Still no rain. "The clouds are so heavy," he said. "A lion's heart is not strong enough for them. You must bring me a baboon. It must be a perfect specimen. without a blemish, and with every hair on its body unhurt."

He chuckled to himself. He knew it would take them many weeks to catch a baboon. At last, battered and bleeding, the men returned with a baby baboon they had caught among the rocks.

"My heart is rent in pieces," said the old rain-maker. "See, there is a scratch here on its ear, and two hairs are missing from its tail. I cannot make rain if even one hair is missing."

The people began to get angry. Why did not rain come? Moffat rang the bell for evening worship in the chapel. "That is the cause of all the trouble," exclaimed the rain-maker. "The white man's bell frightens the rain away. When rain-clouds come over, the white men look at them, and the clouds take fright and go away."

Things looked black for the missionaries. That night, before going to bed, Moffat read aloud from the Bible: "The Lord of hosts is with us; the God of Jacob is our refuge." Then unafraid they lay down to sleep.

"Mr. Hamilton and I will look on the ground," Moffat told the people next day. "Then the clouds will not be frightened at our white faces and my black beard."

At last the people of the tribe lost patience with the rain-maker. They had given him their best sheep and cattle, and had carried out his commands, and still there was no rain. They decided to kill him.

Moffat strode into their midst, and pleaded for

his life. "He could not bring rain because he is a man, and not God," said Moffat. "If you kill him, you will be guilty of murder."

One of the leading elders stood up in a great rage, quivering his spear. "Our people and herds are dying, the rain-maker has eaten our cattle. I shall plunge this spear into his heart. Who are you to stop me?"

"I will give a ransom if need be to save his life," said Moffat. "But he is our enemy," they cried. "I have told you that Jesus died to save His enemies," Moffat answered.

The people were puzzled and angry, but reluctantly they let the rain-maker go.

*   *   *

Moffat had saved his life, but he felt no nearer to the Bechuana people. They would not give him trust or friendship.

"Things will not improve till I know their language," said Moffat. "I am sure of it."

"You never get time to learn it here," said Mary.

"The only way will be to go and live alone in one of the villages," replied Robert, "and listen and talk, and write down the words as I learn them. But I do not like leaving you alone, here, Mary."

52

Mary did not like it either. She was often afraid. But she did not mean Robert to know. She was sure that God would take care of her and her babies, and help her to be brave. There were two children in the mission house now, Mary who was two years old, and Ann who was not yet one. The natives called Robert and Mary Ra-Mary and Ma-Mary—father and mother of Mary—as soon as the first baby was born.

7

RESCUE

AT last Moffat persuaded Chief Mothibi to agree to move to more fertile land. Some years before Moffat had seen the spring of water at Kuruman. It was one of the purest springs of water in the world, and it never failed. There might be drought all around, but there would still be water in the Eye of Kuruman. He determined to build the new mission station there.

He needed new stocks of seeds and tools. He had been in the wilds now for four years, and his stocks were exhausted. So he and the family went down in the wagon to Cape Town.

There were five children in the wagon—Mary and Ann Moffat, and two little Bushmen children whom Moffat had rescued from death, and Peclo, the son of Chief Mothibi. It was the first time any of the children had been in a city, or seen shops, streets, carriages, and the sea.

They took back with them seeds and tools, food and medicines. There was much to be done to prepare the new mission station. Hamilton, the missionary-builder, hewed out blocks of stone from the rocks, to build a church and a house for the missionaries. Meanwhile the Moffats went on working at Lattakoo till the new buildings were ready at Kuruman.

Mary Moffat was teaching little Mary and Ann and the two Bushmen children to sew and read. Mary and Ann talked Sechuana as easily as English. They thought the world was a place where the sun always shone. They had hardly ever seen rain. When a shower did come, they were so excited that they used to run out and stand in it to get wet.

Still the thieving and lying went on at Lattakoo. Moffat was sometimes in despair, but Mary never lost hope. Sometimes when the little African children fell into the fire, or upset the cooking pot on themselves, or cut their knees, they would let Ma-Mary bandage them up. "One day they will come to trust us," she said, "and learn to know God's love."

*   *   *

News spread round the villages by bush telegraph of the strange happenings at Lattakoo. Robert and Mary did not know how the messages were sent. Sometimes they heard the native drums throbbing in strange rhythms. Faintly in the distance would come an answering drum. Sometimes an African climbed on the top of a kopje and shouted, and his voice carried for miles in the clear air. Groups of natives went far afield chasing game for food, and met others on the way. In all these ways news spread.

One day an African, back from hunting, brought a message. "The people of the crocodile, the Bangwaketse, would like you to visit them. They want to know what you are teaching the people at Lattakoo. They would like to learn too."

Robert was worried. "I think I should go, Mary," he said. "It is an opportunity to tell these people of the Gospel. But I don't like leaving you and the children here alone. Hamilton is busy at Kuruman. You will be the only white people here."

"Of course you must go, Robert," said Mary. "The Lord will watch over us. I shall not be anxious."

But she watched him go with a sinking heart. She was desperately afraid, but she was determined no one should know. She prayed silently to God for courage, and went about her work as usual.

"When is father coming back?" asked the children.

56

"We must not be impatient," said Ma-Mary. "He will come back as soon as he has finished his work."

She knew he would return at once if he thought that she was afraid, so she wrote him a letter giving him good news of herself and the children and the station, and hoping he was looking after his cough.

She gave the letter to a native runner. "Take this to the master," she said. "If you take it quickly, and bring me back an answer from him, you shall have a reward."

The man started off eagerly. Two days later he was back. He held out to Mary a piece of blood-stained linen. "The master is dead," he said. "He has been killed. This is a piece of his shirt." He held out his hands for his reward. Sick at heart, Mary gave him tobacco and beads. She turned the rag over and over. Yes, it was Robert's. There was the patch she herself had sewn. Even then she could not believe that Robert was dead.

A week later the children rushed up to Mary. "Look at the cloud of dust, Mother! Someone is coming. Perhaps it is Father." Mary hardly dared to look. But a few minutes later she heard a strong deep voice. Robert was back!

That night she showed him the blood-stained

rag, torn from his shirt. "Yes, I remember," he said. "One of the Griquas cut his finger, and I tore a bit off my shirt for a bandage. The messenger must have got it from him, and brought it back to you to get his reward quickly, without bothering to look for me. How anxious you must have been, Mary!"

*   *   *

It was a glad day when Robert Hamilton rode over to tell the Moffats that the new mission house at Kuruman was ready, and they could move in.

Some weeks later, Mary was just shutting the door of the new house one Sunday morning to keep out stray hens and snakes and cattle while she went across to morning service. One of the native servants was with her.

"There's a baby crying," said the servant casually.

"Where?" asked Ma-Mary.

"Up on the hillside," said the woman. "They buried it early this morning. Its mother died."

"Show me the place," said Mary fiercely. Turning her back on the church, she made the amused woman hurry to a pile of stones on the hill. As they drew near, she could hear a whimpering sound. One or two others joined them to see what this strange white woman would do next. She made them help her tear away the stones. There buried underneath, was a naked brown baby girl, just five weeks old. Mary Moffat had just lost her own baby boy who had only lived for five days. All babies were precious to her. She picked up the little thing, still alive and crying, and carried it home. When Robert came back from church, wondering why Mary had not been there, he found his family increased by one.

"What shall we call her?" asked Mary. "I think Sarah is a good name." "And Roby after the minister who led me to be a missionary," said Robert. So Sarah Roby was christened, and joined the other children in the mission house.

8

FLIES AND INK

"LOOK, Ann, this is how you make the pattern. Lena showed me."

Mary and Ann were sitting under a shady bush outside the mission house at Kuruman. A cat lay stretched out in the sand beside them. Lena, who was a Chief's daughter, had been staying with them, so that Mrs. Moffat could teach her to read and sew and cook. She made beautiful baskets, woven from reeds and grasses which she dyed herself, and she had taught young Mary to make them too.

They looked up as they heard the steady klop klop of oxen's hooves. "That sounds like our wagon," exclaimed Mary. "I hope Father has come back."

They ran to meet it, then paused. "Who's that dirty old man getting down?" asked Ann. "He looks as though he never washed. His clothes smell, too."

Their dog rushed past them, and jumped up at the man, wagging his tail with delight. "It *is*

Father," cried Mary. He waved to them, and called out a greeting in Sechuana.

"Where have you been, Father?" Mary asked.

"Let me get clean first, and then I'll tell you," he said. He turned and spoke to the servants, and then went ahead to the house.

"Did you hear how quickly he talked?" whispered Mary. "It sounded just like one of the natives talking. He's been staying in their huts to learn the language."

*   *   *

Ann climbed up on to his knee before bedtime. "Tell us about it," she begged.

"It is hard to talk English again," said Robert Moffat. "I have spoken nothing but Sechuana for ten weeks. I stayed in a village two hundred miles away from here. We saw lions and giraffes and rhino. I shot a rhino for food, and the natives were so hungry and excited that they thrust their spears into its hide and were going to tear it apart for food. The old rhino was furious. He was not dead at all, and he got to his feet and tore up the ground with his horn, and they ran away in terror.

"I lived in one of those little beehive huts that you have seen so often. I had to crawl in through the door because it was so low. Nobody in the village had ever seen soap, and there wasn't any water to spare for washing. The natives never washed their skin or clothes, and I couldn't wash either."

"But you have been away for ten weeks," exclaimed young Mary, horrified.

"Yes," said Robert. "Your mother thinks she will have to burn my shirt. She doesn't think she can ever get it clean again. We ate with our fingers and insects dropped down into the food. Night-time was the worst because the insects used to bite most then, and spiders dropped down from the roof of the hut on to my face when I was in bed, and snakes crawled over my feet. I went wherever the natives went, and listened to them talking, and asked them questions, and wrote down the names for things as soon as I learnt them."

He showed the children the book in which he had written down words and sentences. "It looks like the grammar book Mother has been making me learn," said Mary.

"This is going to be a grammar book one day," Robert explained. "The very first grammar in the Sechuana language. Now I know the words and the grammar, I can start translating the Bible into Sechuana, and the people will be able to read it for themselves."

Mary Moffat, who was busy patching the children's clothes, looked up with shining eyes. "That will be a great day, Robert," she remarked.

"Why is your writing so smudgy, Father?" asked Ann.

"That is where the flies walked over it," he replied. "Sometimes the whole paper was covered with them. As soon as I dipped my pen in the inkhorn, flies sat on the pen to drink up the ink, and as fast as I wrote a word on the paper, the flies followed the letters to drink up some more. I couldn't write at all at night, because as soon as I lit a candle, flies and moths flew into it and put it out.

"The people were always hungry, and when I shot an animal for the pot they danced and shrieked and sang all night. I tried to talk to them about God, but I could not make them understand. They just laughed. They thought God was a kind of rain-maker. But when they can read the Bible for themselves, they will begin to understand."

*   *   *

Before Mary and Ann settled down to sleep that night, they heard the sounds of a violin. It was Robert Moffat, playing a Scots psalm tune on his fiddle.

"It's nice to have Father home again," murmured Ann.

"I hope he doesn't have to go away again for a long time," added Mary. "Mother worries when he's away, although she pretends she doesn't."

"Perhaps he will stay with us all the time now," said Ann sleepily. "With you and me and Robert and Helen and Mother."

9

"BAYETE! BAYETE!"

FOR a little while Ann thought her wish was coming true. Her father and mother were kept very busy at Kuruman. Her mother had a school now for the children of the village, and taught them to read and write and wash and sew. Young Mary was learning to help her mother with making candles and soap, and looking after the babies.

Robert found it difficult to get time for translation. He had to dig deep furrows to bring the water from the spring to the gardens at Kuruman, so that the villagers could grow food. He had to teach and preach and visit the sick and dying, pull out teeth, and settle quarrels. He had to mend shoes for himself and his family—to go pioneering through the bush—to keep the wagon in repair and tend the oxen.

Little by little a change came over the Africans who lived in Kuruman. Six of them asked Moffat to teach them more about Jesus. One day they came to him and said they wanted to follow

Jesus, and Moffat baptized them, together with his own baby. "We must be clean if we are followers of Jesus," they said, and they stopped painting their bodies with red ochre, and threw away their dirty cloaks of animal skin. The men wanted to wear shirts and trousers like Robert Moffat, and the women wanted cotton dresses. Mary Moffat was the only white woman in Kuruman, and she had to keep stopping her work to show an African woman how to sew a hem or put in a sleeve. Sometimes a man would go about with a trouser on one leg because he had not yet got enough material for a second one, or his wife did not know how to join two legs together.

"We must build a school for Ma-Mary," said the new Christians. "She teaches our children in the hot sun, and the dust makes her cough." They got busy, and made mud bricks and dried them out of doors, and built Ma-Mary her very first school-house.

*   *   *

One day a native carrier brought a box to the mission house. Parcels came so seldom that the children crowded round to see what was in it. Mary lifted out a picture. "That is your grandfather," she said, "and here is grandmother." In excitement they hung them up on the bare walls of the mission house. Next came a silver cup packed in shavings.

Robert lifted it out, and then felt further down in the box.

"Why!" he exclaimed, "it's a silver communion set. We are having out first communion service tomorrow. How wonderful that this has come just in time. Whoever knew we were wanting one?"

"I wrote home for it months ago," said Mary. "I knew we should need it one day."

All was quiet at the mission house next day as the new Christians took part with Robert and Mary in the first communion service ever held at Kuruman.

As soon as the service was over, there was a knock on the door. "Ra-Mary, two strangers have arrived and wish to speak to you," said one one of the Kuruman natives.

Moffat stepped outside. There facing him were two tall Zulu warriors, each carrying a long spear and a pointed oval shield made of buffalo hide. They wore aprons of monkey-tails, and necklaces of lions' teeth round their necks, while their feather headdresses stirred in the breeze. Behind them stood their servants.

"We come from Chief Mzilikazi, the Lion's

Paw, the King of Heaven. Mzilikazi wants to know about the white man's camp at Kuruman."

"Do you come as friends?" asked Moffat.

"We come as friends," replied the warriors, handing their spears to their servants as a sign of peace.

Chief Mzilikazi was the most powerful Chief in Southern Africa. By raid and battle he had conquered the surrounding tribes. He wanted to find out what was happening at Kuruman.

The Bechuana were amazed to see Moffat walking round unafraid with the fierce Zulu warriors, showing them the store with goods in it such as they had never seen, the carpenter's bench, the blacksmith's shop, the flourishing gardens, the school and the church.

"We go to tell the Chief what we have seen," they said. "But our enemies know we are here, and will lie in wait for us. Will Mynheer come with us, so that we may travel in safety?"

*   *   *

"Father is off on his travels again," said Ann to little Robert.

"I wish I could go with him," sighed young Mary. "I would like to see Mzilikazi and his court."

Mary did not know then how much of her life would be spent in wagons as the wife of David Livingstone, the missionary explorer.

"I wish he would stay here," said Ann. "But I know he must go."

For days Moffat and the Matabele warriors journeyed through burnt and blackened villages destroyed by Mzilikazi's warriors, and through villages where the inhabitants fled in terror when they saw the dreaded Zulu spear and shield.

Every Sunday Moffat went a little way from the camp for prayer, remembering those who would be worshipping at Kuruman at the same time. "Mynheer is Sundaying," said the warriors, and left him undisturbed.

When they came in sight of the smoke from the cooking fires at Mzilikazi's kraal, the warriors halted. "We must wait for permission to enter," they said. "There dwells Mzilikazi, the Lord of Heaven, the Elephant, the Lion's Paw."

Permission was given, and Moffat rode alone into the midst of the kraal. In a wide open space in the centre of the kraal stood eight hundred warriors—with spears, shields, and feather head-dresses—motionless. Moffat felt that he was riding into a ring of copper statues. They were so still and silent that they hardly seemed to breathe.

He could feel his own breath coming quickly. How would Mzilikazi receive him? He prayed for courage as he rode steadily forward. His guard led him into the centre of the circle, and told him to dismount. As he put his foot to the ground, the statues suddenly came to life with a wild yell. Three hundred more warriors leapt up from the cover of the bushes. All lowered their spears and pointed them at Moffat, and crouched and swayed towards him, shouting their battle-cry, "Bayete! Bayete!"

Then, at a word of command, the warriors froze again into statues. Their ranks parted. Through them came a tall, dignified Chief, clad in magnificent leopard-skins.

"Mzilikazi!" said the chief of command, kneeling at his feet.

He beckoned his interpreter, who crouched low at his feet till the Chief told him to stand.

Mzilikazi and Moffat looked fearlessly into each other's eyes. Mzilikazi felt that he had met his equal.

"My heart is white as milk," he said.

"My heart is gentle as a dove," replied Moffat.

"I live today by the stranger of another nation," continued the Chief. "You have protected me and saved me from my enemies."

70

"But I have never seen you till today, O Chief," said Moffat, puzzled.

"These two indunas are my eyes and ears." As he spoke, the Chief pointed out the two warriors whom Robert had brought safely back from Kuruman. "What you did to them, you did to me. I shall call you Machobane. That was my father's name, and you shall be a father to me."

Just then Moffat heard a familiar creaking, rumbling sound. His men were driving the ox-wagon into the village. Mzilikazi's eyes grew wide-open with surprise. He stared and stared. "What is that?" he demanded. It was the first time in his life that he had seen a wheel.

He seized Moffat's wrist, and pulled him along to the wagon. Moffat demonstrated how a wheel was made—the hub and the spokes and the iron tyre. The oxen were out-spanned. Mzilikazi called some of his braves, who came and knelt before him.

"Take the shafts and pull," he ordered, "so that I may see these strange things turning. You must teach my people too to make wheels," he said to Moffat. He overcame his fears and climbed inside the strange house on wheels, looking at everything that was in it.

*   *   *

Moffat watched Mzilikazi as he dealt with offenders in his court. An officer was brought before him who had broken one of the unimportant rules of the tribe.

"Let him die," pronounced Mzilikazi without hesitation. A warrior stepped forward to spear him.

"Let him live, O Chief," broke in Moffat.

The warriors waited to see Moffat himself struck down, but the Chief never moved.

"My friend has spoken," said Mzilikazi. "I allow you to live."

"The Lord of Heaven wishes to save men, not to kill them," went on Moffat.

"I am the Lord of Heaven," said the puzzled Chief.

"The true Lord of Heaven is your lord too, Mzilikazi," answered the missionary. "When I come again I will bring you a book which will help you to understand."

"Now surely the Lion's Paw will kill him for his words," murmured the warriors. "He stands upright before him too and does not kneel."

But the Chief and the missionary trusted each other. "I do not understand, Moshete," said the Chief. Moshete was the nearest he could get to saying Moffat, and it was his favourite name for the missionary. "You must teach me and help me to understand."

72

"I will come again, Mzilikazi," said Moffat as he rode away eight days later.

"I shall welcome you always, Moshete," replied the Chief as the wagon rumbled away on its long journey back to Kuruman.

10

THE KRAAL OF THE LION'S PAW

MZILIKAZI soon learnt that not all white men were like Moshete. Some white men killed his herdsmen and stole his cattle. The chief's warriors, shouting their battle cry "Bayete", fought back. White men were now enemies.

One day Dr. Smith, an explorer, arrived at Kuruman, with seven ox-wagons and red-coated soldiers to protect him. He looked hard at Moffat. As well as doing all the ordinary duties of a missionary, Moffat had been working by day and far into the night on his translation work. His head was buzzing, and he had a high temperature and fever. He had been eighteen years now in Africa. "I am going to send you home to England," said the doctor. "You are a sick man, and you must have a holiday."

"You are going into danger, doctor," replied Moffat. "Mzilikazi will think you have come to attack him. I myself will take you to him. The journey will be a holiday for me."

*　　*　　*

For three weeks they travelled. Each night they out-spanned and made a *laager* with the wagons—the front wheels of each wagon touching the wheels of the one before, strips of leather tied round the outside to make a fence, and brushwood stuffed in between the wheels. Men and horses stayed inside the wagon circle, and the oxen were tethered outside.

One day they came to a patch of bare burnt earth. "We are near the Chief now," said Moffat. "He does that to protect his kraal. He leaves no grass for men to hide in or for cattle to eat."

When it was dark, five warriors appeared silently at the camp. "Mzilikazi would see Ra-Mary alone," they said.

"I will ride on and greet the Chief and tell him that you are my friends," said Moffat to Dr. Smith and the soldiers.

The red coats watched the missionary ride off alone next morning to the kraal of the Lion's Paw.

"He's a brave fellow," said one of the men. "I thought he was hard when he fined us sticks of tobacco when we swore, but I wish I'd got half his courage."

"Did you hear what he was singing by the camp fire after we out-spanned last night?" asked another.

"E'en though I walk through death's
      dark vale,
  Yet will I fear none ill;
  For Thou art with me, and Thy rod
  And staff me comfort still.

I learnt that when I was a boy, but I had forgotten it. That's his secret, lads."

*   *   *

When the explorer's wagons drew up at Mzilikazi's kraal some hours later, Dr. Smith saw two men sitting side by side on a leopard-skin rug. In front of them was set out a meal of meat, wild fruit, and calabashes of milk. Chief Mzilikazi had one arm round the shoulders of his friend, Ra-Mary, and with his other hand he stroked Moffat's fine black beard. He hated other invaders of his tribe, but Ra-Mary was his friend.

After introducing the scientist-explorer and his party, Moffat had other news for the Chief. A party of American missionaries was coming to start work among Mzilikazi's tribe. Would the Chief receive them kindly?

"If they are friends of Ra-Mary, they will be friends of mine," said the Chief. "I will give them a place to live, and they shall teach my people."

Moffat told the Chief about the big stone church which he and Hamilton, the missionary-builder, and Millen the missionary-stonemason, were putting up at Kuruman. "We need trees to make the roof beams," said Moffat. "Big trees. We have no big trees near Kuruman."

"You may have all the trees you need from my lands," said the Chief.

Moffat stayed at the royal kraal for two months, and then made his way back to Kuruman. It was with a glad heart that he told the new American missionaries on their way north that a welcome awaited them at Mzilikazi's kraal. Native hunters brought news back to Moffat of the change that was coming over the Matabele, Mzilikazi's warriors. They were learning from the missionaries to live at peace with one another, and to build instead of to destroy.

*   *   *

Then one day came terrible news. A party of Boers (Dutch farmers) were trekking up north from Cape Colony. They wanted to rid themselves of the warlike Matabele who blocked their way.

As smoke was going up from the cooking pots in the kraal of the Lion's Paw, there came the whistle of a bullet from a Boer gun, then another and another. The warriors seized their spears and shields and rushed forward to attack, but a hail of bullets mowed them down. As the mission doctor bent over the bedside of a sick missionary down with fever, a bullet pinged through the hut and made a hole in the wall.

The Boers were amazed to find white men in the village. They dragged them out to safety, while other Boers captured six thousand Matabele cattle.

Moffat was aghast when he heard the news. "Where is the Lion's Paw?" he asked.

"No one knows," he was told. "His kraals are destroyed. He has gone into hiding. No man can find him."

"The missionaries were teaching us to live in peace," they lamented. "They told us that Christians did not fight each other. Why does the British Queen let white men fight? She should tell them to live at peace too."

*   *   *

Moffat was sick at heart. He was worn out with his work at his home-made printing press.

It was time for the translation of the New Testament to be revised, and the British and Foreign Bible Society were willing to print it for him if he would bring the manuscript to London and show them how to set up type for the Sechuana language. He had been away from home for twenty-two years. His children had never seen England or Scotland. The doctors had told him that he would collapse unless he had a break, and the Directors of the Missionary Society in London urged him to come.

He waited until the new church at Kuruman was finished and opened, in November, 1838. Such a big building had never been seen north of the Orange River. Eight hundred natives crowded in for the opening service, and one hundred and fifty baptized Christians stayed to communion.

Then the business of loading up the wagons for the trek down to Cape Town began. There were six Moffat children now. The two Bushmen children and Sarah Roby were staying in Kuruman.

In the wagon, Moffat read some papers which had been sent out to him from England. "They say it is the fashion now in England for men to shave off their beards," he told the family. His beard, the pride and joy of the Lion's Paw, was long and curly. One day when the wagons halted, he slipped away behind a bush, and came back without it. "Look at Father!" laughed the children. "How different he looks. The Chief wouldn't know him now!"

11

WELCOME HOME

"LOOK, Jack! that's one of the new tugs. It's got no oars or sails. It goes by steam. Look at the black smoke coming out of the funnel."

The ship which had brought home soldiers from China and the Moffats from Cape Town was sailing up the river Thames in the summer of 1839. The voyage from Cape Town had lasted three months. Three days out to sea, Jim Moffat, aged three, had died, just after his baby sister had been born on board. Mary, Ann, Robert, Helen and Jack leant over the ship's rail for their first sight of England, while Mrs. Moffat held the baby in her arms.

Mrs. Moffat's father was still alive. The children knew what he looked like because of the picture on the wall at Kuruman. One of the new railways—the Manchester to Liverpool—which was only a few years old, ran near his house. Mary and Ann took the children to see it. "Doesn't it make our old wagon seem slow?" said Robert.

People in the churches in Britain were anxious

to hear about the mission in Africa, and Moffat travelled all over the country by stage coach to address meetings. There was a young Scots medical student at one of his meetings. He came up to Moffat afterwards. "I was going to China as a missionary," he said. "But there is war there, and no foreigners are allowed to enter. Do you think I could be of use anywhere else?"

Robert Moffat looked at him. "Africa needs men like you. I have seen in the morning sun the smoke of a thousand villages where no missionary has ever been. We could do with you in Africa. What is your name?"

"David Livingstone," replied the student.

Some months later, Mrs. Moffat wrote a letter to Robert Hamilton the builder, who was still at Kuruman. "Two new missionaries are coming out," she told him, "both Scotchmen and plain in their manners." Their names were William Ross and David Livingstone. Ross was married, but Livingstone was a bachelor. "I have done what I could to persuade Livingstone to marry, but he seems to decline it," she added.

*   *   *

The Moffats stayed in England for three

years. Moffat saw his New Testament through the press, and wrote a book, *Labours and Scenes in South Africa*. They lived on Brixton Hill in London. Moffat had so much speaking to do that sometimes he seemed away from home almost as much as he did in Africa.

When the ship *Fortitude* set sail from Gravesend, they all felt that they were going home again. They had ten weeks' stormy sailing to Cape Town, then changed on to a small coastal boat for Port Elizabeth (Algoa Bay). Then the baggage had to be loaded on to ox-wagons for the slow journey up country to Kuruman. "Isn't it slow after the stage coaches and the railway?" said the boys.

They crossed the Orange River on a pontoon bridge. They were getting excited now—Kuruman was getting nearer every hour. "Look!" said Mary, "there's someone coming on horseback. Whoever can it be? We're still a hundred miles from home."

"It's young Dr. Livingstone," exclaimed Robert.

The doctor rode up to meet them. "Welcome home!" he said. "All is well at Kuruman."

He rode by the side of the wagon the hundred miles to Kuruman. The school bell and the church bell were ringing in Kuruman to welcome the travellers home. The children had a holiday, and men and women crowded forward to greet the Moffats. The people were neat, tidy and smiling. The gardens were well-kept. Moffat noticed men who were old enemies coming out together to greet him. The God of peace had made them friends.

Moffat and Livingstone talked together by candlelight. Livingstone told him how the Boers had advanced up country and wiped out native villages.

"It must be the Bible and the plough for Africa," said Moffat. "I want to teach the people to love God and read their Bibles, and to grow food for themselves so that they can live at peace with one another, and have no need to fight."

"I will go anywhere provided it be forward," said Livingstone.

*   *   *

Livingstone rode away back to his mission station, and the Moffats wondered when they would see him again. The next meeting was sooner than they expected. One day two months later they saw a white-faced, shaken man being helped along to the mission house at Kuruman. His left arm was in a sling.

84

"Why, David, whatever has happened?" said Mrs. Moffat, hurrying out to greet him.

"Don't worry," said David. "It was a lion. He got me by the shoulder, and crushed the bones. I should have been a dead man but for Mebalwe who was with me. He shot at the lion and it let me go. The bones are knitting already —I shall be fit again soon."

The Moffats nursed Livingstone back to health and strength at Kuruman. Mary, a pioneer's daughter herself, thrilled with David's plans for fighting the slave trade, and taking the Gospel forward into the heart of Africa. She and David knew that they would be happy together, and it was a day of rejoicing at Kuruman when they were married, and set off in the wagon for Mary's new home at Mabotsa.

12

FAREWELL TO THE CHIEF

MOFFAT often wondered about the Lion's Paw. Was he still in hiding? Had he reassembled his scattered tribe of warriors and started life afresh?

There was war now in the land. The Livingstones had moved to Kolobeng. Then came news that the mission station there had been burnt and destroyed by the Boers. Livingstone blazed with anger. He determined to open up a trail across Africa where black men and white could travel in safety, free from slave-trader or Boer raider. He sent Mary and their babies home to Britain, and he tramped away into the unknown hinterland. He had been gone a long time now, and no news had come of him. What had happened to him too, Ra-Mary wondered.

At last Moffat could wait no longer. Two white traders had arrived at Kuruman and asked Moffat if he would travel with them, as they were afraid to go farther north alone. The country was still at war. Would Kuruman be attacked and destroyed as Kolobeng had been? Moffat hoped not. He talked things over with Mary, and as usual she urged him to go.

"David will be needing stores wherever he is," she said. "I will pack some up for you." Into one of the packages she slipped a note, "Prayer, unceasing prayer, is made for you."

"I must take a present for the Lion's Paw," said Moffat. Just then one of the young Moffats called to his father to come and see their cat with her new kittens. "Mzilikazi has never seen a tame cat," said Moffat. Mary and the children agreed that a kitten would make a splendid present for the Chief.

*   *   *

At Shoshong, Moffat asked Chief Sechele to give him guides. He was heading for a piece of country that he had never travelled in before. But Sechele was uneasy—he was afraid of the white men in the south, and of Mzilikazi and his Matabele. He refused to give Moffat any help.

Moffat was travelling through unknown country. No one knew where the Lion's Paw was hiding, For eighteen days he and the two white traders travelled by compass only. They had to make their own path—hacking a way through breast-high grass and thorn bushes, cutting down trees, while the wagon wheels struck against hidden boulders.

Then they came to a bare and blackened land, where grass and villages had been destroyed by fire.

"We are in Mzilikazi's domain now," said Moffat. "He burns the land round his own kraal so that there shall be no food or shelter for an attacking enemy."

Some days later they reached the headquarters of the Lion's Paw. The village was still only half-built. Mzilikazi was in no hurry to build villages for the Boers to burn.

Instead of a thousand men motionless before the chief's hut, there were only sixty warriors drawn up in silence. A sub-chief led Moffat forward. No one spoke. He drew back a reed curtain. There sat Mzilikazi, the Lion's Paw, the Elephant, a sick man, huddled on a stool, too ill with dropsy to walk or stand.

"Moshete, Moshete!" he cried. Then he covered his face with his leopard-skin cloak. No one should say they had seen Mzilikazi weep, but he was weeping now, tears of joy that Moshete had come again.

*　　*　　*

Helped by Moffat's medicine, and the joy at seeing him again, Mzilikazi began to mend. When he was better Moffat spoke to him of his plans. "I will do anything you ask, Moshete," said the Chief.

"I want to find my son-in-law, Dr. Livingstone," said Moffat. "I have parcels here for him—food and clothes and medicines that he will need. Can you send scouts to find him?"

The scouts came back disappointed. "We have been as far as the Makololo country," they said. "The Makololo will not let us pass through their territory—the Makololo do not love the Matabele. They will not send out scouts for us. But the Doctor is far away beyond their country. We know that he has passed through there."

"I will go myself to look for him, Chief," announced Moffat.

"We will go together," said the Lion's Paw.

"But, Chief," protested Moffat, "you have been a very sick man. And the Makololo are your enemies."

But Mzilikazi had made up his mind. He summoned his sub-chiefs, and his warriors with their shields and spears. The oxen were harnessed to Moffat's wagon, and the packages for Livingstone stored inside. Lumbering along, at the pace of the oxen, the cavalcade headed northwards towards the great Zambesi river. Some days later, the Chief called a halt.

"We can go no further, Moshete," he said. "My kingdom ends here. Beyond are three enemies—the Makololo, the tsetse fly, and the desert."

Moffat had brought the packages seven hundred miles already, and he was determined to get them through to Livingstone. The Chief agreed to trust them to some of his most faithful men, who carried the goods to the Zambesi. There, on the banks of the river, they left them, calling to the Makololo outposts on an island in midstream that they were for Monare, the doctor. A year later when the missionary stumbled into the outpost, more dead than alive, the goods were safely awaiting him.

Moffat and the Chief were to meet only once more. The Missionary Society planned to send out two parties of missionaries—one to the Matabele, and one to their enemies the Makololo, to teach them the Christian way and to bring them into friendship. Moffat, with his long years of experience and his friendship with the Lion's Paw, led the party of young missionaries to the Matabele. One of the missionaries was his own son, John.

*　　　*　　　*

Mzilikazi loved Moshete, but he did not want any other white men settling among his people. He had learnt to distrust hat-wearers. He was afraid that if he let the missionaries settle, soldiers would follow, and his lands would be taken from him.

It was many weeks before Moffat could persuade the Chief to let the missionaries start work among his people. At last his patience won the day, and his prayers bore fruit. The Chief agreed to let the missionaries stay.

"You will keep my friends here in safety?" Moffat asked.

"Your friends will be safe with my people," replied the Chief. "My heart is all milk."

"Good-bye, my friend," said Moffat. "God's peace rest upon you and your people."

The Chief and the missionary never met again. But Mzilikazi kept his promise, and the tribe after him. Robert Moffat's little grandson was the first white baby to be born among the Matabele people, in what is now known as Zimbabwe.

13

THE LAST TREK

IT was April, 1874. Crowds of people in dark clothes moved quietly forward into Westminster Abbey.

"Who is that tall old man with the white beard?" asked someone.

"That's Robert Moffat of Kuruman. Don't you remember when he preached in the Abbey a year ago, and told us about his mission work in Africa?"

"Of course," said the other. "I remember now. This will be a sad day for him, coming to the funeral of his son-in-law."

Slowly the coffin containing the body of David Livingstone was carried into the Abbey, and placed in its grave near the spot where the Unknown Soldier is buried today.

Moffat was seventy-eight now, and alone, for Ma-Mary had died. He had been called home from Kuruman to see a new edition of the Sechuana Bible through the press. He was too old to return to Africa, but he travelled all over

Britain telling men and women about the work there. The City of London gave a banquet in his honour, at the Mansion House. The Lord Mayor introduced him as a great missionary, and one who knew all about the diamond fields of South Africa.

"I can tell you little about the diamond fields," said Moffat when he stood up to speak. "I went to South Africa to seek jewels of a very different character, namely the natives, in order that they might be made as gems to adorn the Saviour's crown."

In 1882 there was an Electric Exhibition at the Crystal Palace in London. Moffat and many other Londoners flocked to see the wonder of this new source of power and light. Suddenly he saw an African coming towards him.

"This is Ketshwayo," said the steward who brought him. "He cannot speak English. Can you speak to him and make him understand?"

Moffat spoke to him in Sechuana. "Did you know Mzilikazi?" he asked him.

A smile spread over Ketshwayo's face from ear to ear. "Yes, I have served with his son as an induna. Are you—yes, I am sure now—are you his friend Moshete?"

"I am," said Moffat, rejoicing to hear the old name again.

"O Moshete," said Ketshwayo, "this is a glad day. My heart is all milk."

*　　　*　　　*

Next year, at the age of eighty-seven, Robert Moffat died.

In the Bible House in London, where Robert Moffat's Sechuana Bible was prepared for the press, is a memorial window to great translators of the Scriptures. Tyndale, Jerome, Luther and Carey are there, and in their company stands Robert Moffat.

In the Mangwe Pass in Zimbabwe, is a different memorial. Set in concrete are the tracks of a wagon, a dog, a booted and a barefoot man. Part of the inscription reads:

"One hundred years ago the first of the missionaries, hunters and traders passed slowly and resolutely along this way. Honour their memory."

The first two white men to go over the pass were Sam Edwards, trader, and Robert Moffat, friend of the Chiefs.